THINKING ON YOUR FEET

Marlene Caroselli, Ed.D.

A FIFTY-MINUTE™ SERIES BOOK

CRISP PUBLICATIONS, INC.
Menlo Park, California

THINKING ON YOUR FEET

Not related to Think on Your Feet International™

Marlene Caroselli, Ed.D.

CREDITS:
Editor: **Nina Pohl**
Designer: **Carol Harris**
Typesetting: **ExecuStaff**
Cover Design: **Carol Harris**
Artwork: **Ralph Mapson**

Copyright © 1992 Crisp Publications, Inc.
Printed in the United States of America

English language Crisp books are distributed worldwide. Our major international distributors include:

CANADA: Reid Publishing, Ltd., Box 69559—109 Thomas St., Oakville, Ontario Canada L6J 7R4. TEL: (416) 842-4428; FAX: (416) 842-9327

AUSTRALIA: Career Builders, P.O. Box 1051, Springwood, Brisbane, Queensland, Australia 4127. TEL: 841-1061, FAX: 841-1580

NEW ZEALAND: Career Builders, P.O. Box 571, Manurewa, Auckland, New Zealand. TEL: 266-5276, FAX: 266-4152

JAPAN: Phoenix Associates Co., Mizuho Bldg. 2-12-2, Kami Osaki, Shinagawa-Ku, Tokyo 141, Japan. TEL: 3-443-7231, FAX: 3-443-7640

Selected Crisp titles are also available in other languages. Contact International Rights Manager Tim Polk at (800) 442-7477 for more information.

Library of Congress Catalog Card Number 91-76252
Caroselli, Marlene
Thinking On Your Feet
ISBN 1-56052-117-1

This book is printed on recyclable paper with soy ink.

ABOUT THIS BOOK

Thinking On Your Feet is not like most books. It has a unique "self-study" format that encourages a reader to become personally involved. Designed to be "read with a pencil," there is an abundance of exercises, activities, assessments and cases that invite participation.

The objective of *Thinking On Your Feet* is to help readers improve their ability to express themselves in a positive manner in a variety of situations.

Thinking On Your Feet (and the other self-improvement books listed in the back of this book) can be used effectively in a number of ways. Here are some possibilities:

—**Individual Study.** Because the book is self-instructional, all that is needed is a quiet place, some time and a pencil. By completing the activities and exercises, a reader can achieve skills that lead to significant memory improvement.

—**Workshops and Seminars.** The book is ideal for reading prior to a workshop or seminar. With the basics in hand, the quality of participation will improve. More time can be spent on concept extensions and applications during the program. The book is also effective when a trainer distributes it at the beginning of a session and leads participants through the contents.

—**Remote Location Training.** Copies can be sent to those not able to attend "home office" training sessions.

—**Informal Study Groups.** Thanks to the format, brevity and low cost, this book is ideal for "brown-bag" or other informal group sessions.

There are other possibilities that depend on the objectives, program or ideas of the user. One thing is for sure, even after it has been read, this book will serve as excellent reference material which can be easily reviewed.

ABOUT THE AUTHOR

Dr. Marlene Caroselli founded the Center for Professional Development in 1984 and since that time has served as a consultant/trainer on both the national and the international levels. Among her corporate/organizational clients are the Department of Defense, the Department of the Interior, the National Park Service, UCLA, Lockheed Aeronautical Systems, Northrop Corporation, Mobil Chemical, the Credit Managers Association, TRW, Dow Precision Hydraulics, Allied-Signal, the U.S. Office of Personnel Management, Xerox Corporation, Security Pacific Bank, Magnavox, Rockwell International and others.

Her recent book, *The Language of Leadership*, was chosen as a main selection for the Executive Program Book Club. Of her work in that book, Lee Iacocca observed, ''I have to confess that I've never stopped to analyze my speaking style as methodically as you have. I'm glad that it seems to stand up to such highly professional scrutiny.''

Her other books include *Total Quality Transformations, Total Quality Training, The New Manager, Meetings that Work, Hiring and Firing, PowerWriting, Quality—Initiated Icebreakers,* and *Communicate with Quality.*

CONTENTS

INTRODUCTION

Once a word has been allowed to escape, it cannot be recalled.   —*Horace*

Open mouth. Insert feet.

If these four words describe your typical speaking style, you are reading the right book! Every single second of every single day, someone somewhere is saying something that will come back to haunt him. At this very moment, words are flying out of someone's mouth and landing awkwardly or embarrassingly on the ears of some listener. If the speaker is just an "average Joe," his careless speech will probably be soon forgotten.

But if the speaker is a nationally recognized figure, the words will be recorded forever in the oral and written records of our history. How long will it take before Americans can forget the "Read My Lips" declaration? How long will it be before our collective memory forgets a presidential candidate's challenge to reporters: "I have nothing to hide. My life is pretty boring—I invite you to follow me around for a day."

In *Thinking on Your Feet,* you will learn to apply proven techniques for expressing yourself—admirably—in any situation. Whether you're being interviewed or conversing with a colleague, whether you're participating in a meeting or speaking before an audience or attending a social function, your new speaking skills will enable you to say what you mean without causing pain to yourself or others.

Real-life situations will be examined so you can have a chance to formulate your own responses. With sufficient practice, you will be able to think rapidly on your feet and speak off the cuff—persuasively and intelligently.

INTRODUCTION (continued)

Situation: Your boss has called you into his office. You don't know why, so you are a little nervous. (You feel the way you used to feel in school when you were called into the principal's office without an apparent reason.)

He asks you to have a seat and then asks, "Are you intelligent?" You, of course, say yes. His next question, though, really throws you. "How do you know you are intelligent?"

Write your response to the boss's question. Write as quickly as you can. Do not stop to revise or edit; do not worry about correct spelling. Remember, in the real world you have very little time to pull your thoughts together in situations like this.

What would you say? _____

_____

_____

_____

_____

_____

_____

_____

_____

Ask co-workers to respond to the same situation. Then compare their answers to your own. (Do this with all the exercises in the book.) If you think someone has a better answer than yours, examine it to see why it sounds more articulate or more convincing.

By the way, the young woman who had been asked this question by her boss responded in the following way: "To me, 'intelligence' means 'knowledge.' And I know more today than I did yesterday." Do you think that was a good answer? Why or why not?

Here is another opportunity to see how well you would respond in a highly charged situation.

> ***Situation:*** Imagine that you are a secretary who has just disclosed that she has had a romantic relationship with a world-famous figure. The news media has gone wild with their coverage of this scandal and you are constantly being sought for interviews, which you are happy to give, since you've decided to leave the secretarial world anyway and enter show business.
>
> During one of the interviews, a reporter comments that a number of people who know you have stated that you are not a very intelligent person. Then the reporter asks, "How do you respond to that charge?"
>
> What would you say? _____
>
> _____
>
> _____
>
> _____
>
> _____
>
> _____
>
> _____
>
> _____
>
> _____
>
> _____

INTRODUCTION (continued)

There is no guarantee that you will *always* come up with an answer as good as the first example or that you will *never* say something you may later regret. (In the second situation, the young woman replied, ''I am not a *bimbo*!'' Unfortunately, the very use of the word ''bimbo'' somehow suggests ''bimbo-ism.'')

We can, however, assure you that the likelihood of foot-in-mouth-insertion will be greatly diminished if you follow the recommendations at the end of every section, and if you practice the exercises designed to make cogent thoughts roll trippingly off your tongue—even if you haven't had a great deal of preparation time.

In this book, you will explore ways that will help you speak with confidence— whether you have an audience of one or one thousand. And, you will study techniques to enable you to handle virtually any public situation involving interpersonal communications. Thinking on your feet is not a mysterious talent possessed by golden-tongued orators. Rather, it is an acquired skill that almost anyone can learn.

SECTION

I

Being Interviewed

BEING INTERVIEWED

Speech is a mirror of the soul: as a man speaks, so is he. —*Publilius Syrus*

Unless you were born rich, married well, won the lottery or were cited as the prime benefactor in Aunt Bessie's will, you will probably have to work for a living. And since much of the period between our teen-age years and our retirement years is spent on the job, the process of finding the right one is a critically important task.

The Cost of Poor Interviews

Handling the employment interview well can help you find "the perfect job." Not handling the interview well could cause you to lose that job. Understandably, prospective employers regard the interview as their only opportunity to find out if you are the right person for the job. The employer's time is expensive; she *must* ask penetrating questions—questions designed not to embarrass you but to find out if you have the creativity, quick-wittedness, background, skills and experience needed for the job. If the interviewer fails to learn as much as she can about you, she may have to pay for that failure in the future.

Think about the waste that results from a poor interview:

- The interviewer's time is wasted.

- The interviewee's time is wasted.

- If the wrong person is hired and ultimately leaves the position, the time spent training the person up to the point of his departure walks out the door with him. The time, cost, and involvement of other people in training that person are further sources of waste.

- If security clearances were needed, the time and money spent on them is a total waste.

- If employment agencies were used to obtain applicants, their fees still have to be paid, even if the newly hired person leaves the position after a short time.

- Finally, the company must begin the whole process all over again.

BEING INTERVIEWED (continued)

Non-Typical Interview Questions

You can expect non-typical questions—questions like the following that purposely go beneath the polite veneer of interview situations in order to learn how candidates handle themselves in unexpected situations.

Situation: How many uses can you think of for this folder? (or pen or stapler, et cetera) _____

_____

_____

_____

_____

_____

If you were stranded on a deserted island, and if you could only have two people with you, who would you want those people to be?

_____

_____

_____

_____

_____

_____

When interviewers ask a non-typical question, they are usually expecting a non-typical answer. Most people, stranded on a deserted island, would want to have their loved ones with them. And there is nothing wrong with that. The more practical response, however, would be to have a shipbuilder who would be able to construct a craft so the stranded person could get home to his loved ones. Or perhaps to have a comedian, so the stranded person could be entertained while waiting for the shipbuilder to complete the job.

Typical Questions/Non-Typical Answers

Sometimes, you may be asked a typical question, but the asker will be hoping for a non-typical answer. For example, the most frequently asked interview question is:

Situation: "Tell me about yourself." _____

_____

_____

_____

_____

Most people reply to that question by reiterating everything listed on their resume, a copy of which the interviewer has probably already seen. You may wish to say something that will make you stand out from the crowd of candidates who preceded you.

For example, one young woman, when asked to tell about herself, gave an interesting response. "I suppose you could call me a non-conforming conformist," she declared. The curious interviewer asked her to explain her answer.

She elaborated, "I've not always done what others do or what others expect I will do. When I was in college, for example, I did not join a sorority, although that was the popular thing to do. A lot of tears were shed by young women who didn't get into the sorority of their choice. A lot of time was spent trying to impress the sorority members. I thought all of that was a waste of my time, and so I did volunteer work instead with handicapped children at a nearby medical facility."

In view of the above response, you may wish to do more than recap your resume points. What would you say **now** in response to this question?

Situation: "Tell me about yourself." _____

_____

_____

_____

_____

RECOMMENDATIONS

✔ Remember to do your homework: Learn as much as you can about the company, its products, its policies.

✔ Make certain you have assembled facts/documents/certificates/resume items that are aligned with the requirements for the job you want.

✔ Rehearse at least ten times for the interview by having a friend work with you on the typical interview questions included at the end of this chapter.

✔ Be prepared for non-typical interview questions. When employers ask such challenging questions, they are not necessarily trying to trick you or trap you. They are usually trying to see how well you can think on your feet. This critical skill of being able to respond well to an unanticipated situation or question will help you make decisions better, solve problems more creatively, and lead others more easily. How well did you respond to the non-typical questions presented earlier in this chapter?

MEDIA INTERVIEWS

Dealing with radio, television and/or print media can be intimidating. But not if you are prepared. Interviewers, of course, are usually seeking "juicy" bits of information and if you are not cautious in your remarks, you may provide "juice" that can do irreparable damage to your career. The ancient exhortation to think before you speak will serve you especially well in interview situations.

Many people believe that diplomacy is doing the "nastiest thing in the nicest way." The diplomat, when faced with unexpected questions, keeps in mind the power of words and treats them, and the ideas they convey, with great respect.

> *Situation:* Assume you are a nationally recognized figure who has had a well-publicized dispute with a former employer. You have not concealed your dislike of the man. Your former employer dies unexpectedly and the media ask you to comment on his death. What would you say?

_____

_____

_____

_____

_____

_____

_____

_____

_____

This very situation happened to Lee Iacocca upon the death of Henry Ford, Jr. Mr. Iacocca's response noted that he and Henry Ford had been friends for more years than they had been enemies. He then extended his condolences to the family. In one masterful stroke, he expressed sympathy without appearing to be hypocritical. He avoiding saying he regretted the man's passing and yet gave a gentlemanly and totally appropriate reply.

MEDIA INTERVIEWS (continued)

Never lie in response to a difficult question. The truth you tell may not be the same truth a persnickety reporter was driving toward but it can be a truth that satisfies the question. For example, a great many political pundits and observers have speculated on the political plans of New York's Governor Cuomo. In a recent interview, a reporter asked him directly if he intended to run for the presidency. He neatly deflected the question, but the reporter persisted. ''If you are not running for the presidency,'' she postulated, ''why are you so well-informed about foreign affairs?''

He neatly turned the question around by observing, ''You, too, are well-informed, but that does not mean you are seeking a national office.''

The reporter defended herself by pointing out, ''But I have to ask foreign-policy questions every week.''

''And I have to answer them,'' the Governor commented.

Here is another situation for you to try.

> *Situation:* Assume you are the Secretary of the Navy at the end of World War I. You are presiding over a ceremony honoring the women who have served in the Navy—women who will return to civilian life, now that the war is over. What would be a fitting tribute to these veterans?

_____

_____

_____

_____

_____

_____

_____

_____

Unfortunately, Josephus Daniels, Secretary of the Navy in 1918, paid homage with words that were not very carefully selected. He intoned, ''We will not forget you. As we embraced you in uniform yesterday, we will embrace you without uniform tomorrow.''

RECOMMENDATIONS

✔ Always think before you speak. Ask yourself if the words could come back to haunt you. Train your brain to pay attention to the mental red flags that could be signaling trouble for you or for others.

✔ Answer clearly and succinctly. Look directly into the interviewer's eyes. Do not give more information than is being asked for, unless you are extremely comfortable with the topic or unless a discussion of it poses no possible danger.

✔ Learn to be comfortable with pauses. The verbal vacuum will be filled, if not by you, then by the reporter. Many people are so uncomfortable with silence that they rush into saying something they later regret.

✔ Arm yourself with a plethora of facts. Memorize them or have them on cards, if necessary. The more prepared you are, the more knowledgeable you will appear.

✔ When you can, make connections to the important points you want to stress. Be mindful of those points throughout the interview and repeat them when you naturally can. Make logical transitions, though, not lopsided ones.

✔ Do not hesitate to contradict interviewers who give incorrect data. Many people are so bound by propriety and politeness that they hesitate to contradict.

✔ Learn to say ''no'' and make it sound like ''yes.'' If there are some questions that you feel you must legitimately decline to answer, practice ways of declining without offending. Then, provide related information that you are comfortable releasing so the interviewer is not left empty-handed (or perhaps empty-headed).

For example, if you are not at liberty to discuss certain confidential matters, you might say to the interviewer, ''I am not free to provide information on that issue. However, I can tell you what we are doing as far as the *environment* is concerned.''

Another approach might be ''I am certain you will understand that I cannot speak for our CEO—you may wish, however, to ask her those questions directly. I *can* tell you what we, as a corporation, have done in the past to handle such situations.''

RECOMMENDATIONS (continued)

✔ Be aware of your nonverbal language. Your behavior may be giving messages you don't really intend to send! Strive for congruency between you words and your actions. It won't do much good, for example, to say you are not angry if your face is turning red and you are pounding a desk. The greater the alignment between what you say and what you do, the less likely the chance for misinterpretation.

If your job calls for extensive negotiating, however, you may wish to develop a "poker face," so that you don't reveal everything that you are thinking. If you don't have control over this silent language, you may be telling others things they should not know . . . without ever opening your mouth!

Interviewers are skilled at reading this silent body language. Should they sense you are nervous or uncomfortable with a specific topic, they may well focus on that topic to force you to disclose information that is privileged.

EXERCISES

✍ **1**

Researchers have found that people who are verbally fluid can make better decisions and solve problems more readily than people who lack mastery over words. Such language masters also handle interview questions more admirably—they are able to think on their feet without hesitation or difficulty.

This exercise and the one that follows are often found on I.Q. tests that measure your verbal facility and your ability to see relationships.

As quickly as you can, write down ten words that are related in some way to each of the words presented. For example, if the presented word were "stress," related words might be "blood pressure," "nerves," "work-related," "pressure," "fear," "change," " unknown," "ulcer," "time" and "deadline."

You should be able to complete this exercise in about ten minutes. Time yourself.

1. **Call**	6. **Walk**
2. **Clock**	7. **Question**
3. **Homework**	8. **Show**
4. **Pen**	9. **Cat**
5. **Know**	10. **Spring**

EXERCISES (continued)

✍ **2**

This exercise is similar to the other but operates from the opposite position: you are now being given three words and you have to find the one word that is related somehow to the other three.

Relax. Enjoy the challenge. And don't worry about timing yourself on this one.

Ex:	trunk	family	house	_tree_
1.	up	funeral	ship's	
2.	tug	wings of	games	
3.	language	of beef	tied	
4.	nail	arm	M.C.	
5.	toast	door	fry	
6.	paper	William Blake	Tony	
7.	world	Rockefeller	mollusk	
8.	book	contact electronically	boy	
9.	struck	gaze	light	
10.	nerd	tug	soda	

Answers: 10. jerk, 9. star, 8. page, 7. oyster, 6. tiger, 5. French, 4. hammer, 3. tongue, 2. war, 1. wake

✍ **3**

For the next month or so, spend five minutes each day delivering an impromptu speech on each of the following topics. Impromptu means that you can take no more than a minute to prepare your thoughts. You need not actually deliver this speech to an audience, but you should speak it aloud . . . perhaps while you are in the car driving, or when you are exercising, or eating breakfast, or even—if you dare—to a family member who is willing to listen.

A good general guideline for delivering an impromptu speech (also called an ''extemporaneous'' speech) is to follow the Dale Carnegie recommendation to ''Tell them what you're going to tell them. Then tell them. Then tell them what you told them.'' Your high school English teacher called this technique the five-paragraph essay: Introduction, Body (composed of the three middle paragraphs), and Conclusion. It's a formula that works well for organizing practically all types of information.

Tape record yourself, if possible, to track your progress as the days go by. If you can't do that, keep a simple written record to evaluate your daily efforts. This exercise is one of the very best in the world for developing your ability to think on your feet.

Topics			
Day 1:	values	Day 16:	book
Day 2:	chart	Day 17:	dirty feet
Day 3:	highlight	Day 18:	resort
Day 4:	hotel	Day 19:	meeting
Day 5:	Lincoln	Day 20:	city
Day 6:	video	Day 21:	canal
Day 7:	fun	Day 22:	wine
Day 8:	cast	Day 23:	graduate
Day 9:	swine	Day 24:	fry
Day 10:	fly	Day 25:	general
Day 11:	wig	Day 26:	relief
Day 12:	ointment	Day 27:	potato
Day 13:	preparation	Day 28:	bestseller
Day 14:	oddity	Day 29:	jumbo
Day 15:	king	Day 30:	resistance

EXERCISES (continued)

✍ 4

Practice with the following questions. They are not typical of the questions that would be asked in an interview (unless, perhaps, you are being interviewed by Barbara Walters), but they are provocative questions that will challenge you to marshal your thoughts and present a smooth-flowing, intelligent-sounding response.

Have a friend make up other difficult questions for you and practice responding to them.

1. If you could be any city in the world, which city would you choose and why?

_____

_____

_____

_____

2. What if you were president of this company?

_____

_____

_____

_____

3. What if you were an alien from outer space who had just landed in America for the first time? What would your reaction be?

_____

_____

_____

_____

4. They say there is one good book inside every person. What is the book inside you?

_____

_____

_____

_____

_____

5. Aristotle noted that understanding metaphor is the essence of genius. We don't expect a "genius" answer, but what metaphor would you use for "life"? (Please don't say "Life is a bowl of cherries." It's already been taken.)

_____

_____

_____

_____

_____

6. It has been postulated that if women ruled the world, there would be no wars. In your opinion, what would a world ruled by women be like?

_____

_____

_____

_____

_____

7. What is your favorite word in the English language and why?

_____

_____

_____

_____

EXERCISES (continued)

8. If you suddenly were given the power to be invisible, how would you use that power?

_____

_____

_____

_____

_____

9. What was your last original thought?

_____

_____

_____

_____

_____

10. What product do you think should be on the market but isn't?

_____

_____

_____

_____

_____

S E C T I O N

II

Communicating with Colleagues and Customers

COMMUNICATING WITH COLLEAGUES AND CUSTOMERS

Speak cleverly, if you speak at all; carve every word before you let it fall. —*Oliver Wendell Holmes*

It has been observed by some unknown sage that "the infinite capacity of human beings to misunderstand one another makes our jobs and our lives far more difficult than they have to be." Think about misunderstandings you have had in the past—with family members, with friends, with co-workers or bosses or customers. Most of those misunderstandings probably would not have occurred in the first place if clear and thoughtful communications had preceded the misunderstanding.

It is not easy to communicate well; however, each time you complete a successful exchange of meaning, you should compliment yourself. Then analyze the situation and try to isolate the ingredients that led to success.

Briefly describe the last successful communication interaction you had with another person.

_____

_____

_____

_____

_____

Now comes the tough part. What exactly did you do or say to make the exchange an accurate and significant interaction?

_____

_____

_____

_____

_____

THE COMMUNICATION PROCESS

As far as communicating with others is concerned, we must keep certain things in mind.

- **Communication is irreversible.**

Once a word has left your mouth, there is no calling it back. True, you can attempt to make amends for words you wish you had not uttered, but the initial impact of your words is bound to remain in the receiver's mind for a long time. Thinking well on your feet is truly a matter of *thinking well*—period.

- **Communication is constant.**

You may think you can avoid communicating by being silent. But the truth is, even your silence speaks. It has been said that you cannot *not* communicate. So many aspects of your being are sending out signals or messages to others in the immediate environment. The signals may be misinterpreted, but they are nonetheless being sent.

"Object language," for example, communicates information about the type of person you are by identifying your personal preferences. If you smoke or don't smoke, if you drive a Porsche or a Volkswagen, if you wear designer suits or less formal attire, if you bite your nails or smile excessively—all of the choices you have made or habits you have formed are conveying information about you to other people.

Someone walking into your home could look at the books you have on your bookshelf and probably form a fairly accurate impression of you. The way you have decorated your home or your office is another source of data about the kind of person you are. While you can never escape communicating, you *can* make choices about what symbols you wish to use in the process of communicating. Part of your success in responding easily to unanticipated questions or events will depend on the messages you send—messages that use words as well as those that do not.

- **Communication connects us.**

We may not wish to have any connection formed at all, but communication between two individuals creates a bonding, if only for that instant of their meeting. As a rule, the bonding extends far beyond the casual connections that are made between two strangers.

In the workplace, we are inextricably bound to others in our immediate environment. We may not especially like some of these people and we may try to minimize our encounters with them, but the fact remains there is a symbiotic relationship among individuals who work together.

Recognizing that we are joined to achieve a mutual goal and not to cause friction will help us to achieve some degree of harmony. A spoken reminder of this mutual goal will help reduce conflict.

• **Communication can always be improved.**
In both your professional and your personal activities, you may encounter people who are supremely self-confident and perhaps a little stubborn. You may not feel comfortable around such individuals at first, but with a little practice, you will soon be able to ''hold your own in time.''

Even the best communicators seek to improve their communication style. They revise their words, they practice what they will say, they ask others for feedback, they learn new words, they study the style of people they admire. In short, they are continually looking for ways to hone their words so their messages will be properly carved and clearly understood.

Don't expect to think well on your feet every time you need to. Seek opportunities that will help you sharpen your verbal skills. If you do make a mistake or say something inappropriate, learn from the experience and exercise greater caution the next time. Watch how others handle tense situations and imitate their style.

COMMUNICATING WITH COLLEAGUES

If this were an ideal world, there would be no need for a book like this. But, alas, there will always be some people in your work environment who seem to put you on the spot—either because they enjoy seeing you squirm or perhaps because they simply have a personality that intimidates people. The latter type is easier to deal with.

When you know that a superior or colleague is just gruff by nature, when you know that he does not mean you harm but rather simply expects quick answers backed by competent research, you can be prepared for that expectation.

Hostile colleagues are much more difficult to deal with, for they are operating from psychological drives that may be foreign to you. If you are not used to dealing with sarcasm or put-downs or plain rudeness, you will have to sharpen your defenses in order to reduce the stress such people can cause.

It is important that you keep in mind the ultimate purpose of the interaction in which you are engaged. Especially in your business relationships, shouting, sarcasm or belittling comments will not help you reach your mutual goal. Being angry or sarcastic in response to negative comments will only escalate the anger and take both parties further and further away from their objective.

Before we begin considering what works best with such individuals, consider the dilemma of an American businessman named Brad who had been sent by his company to London to open a new office. The company had given him a letter of introduction to an exclusive men's club in the city. When Brad visited the club it was everything he had imagined it would be, complete with a distinguished-looking older gentleman seated at the next table. Brad was eager to strike up a conversation and so invited the gentleman to join him in a glass of sherry.

The old man declined, saying that he had tried alcohol once and it had such an adverse effect on him that he vowed never to indulge again. They chatted for a few moments and then Brad made another overture of friendship: he offered the other man a cigar.

Again, the Englishman declined, explaining that as a youngster he had tried smoking once and it had made him deathly ill. Since that awful, choking experience, he had never again tried smoking. Brad was undaunted and continued chatting with the man. In a final gesture of goodwill, Brad invited the other man to a game of cards. This time, too, the older man declined, citing the fact that he and his wife had tried to play cards one evening but had found it so frightfully boring that they decided they would never again waste their time with such a diversion.

Noting the crestfallen look on Brad's face, the Englishman quickly made an offer. "I know I'm not much in the way of companionship," he apologized, "but don't despair! My son will be coming by the club soon. Perhaps he will join you."

"Your only child, I presume," Brad remarked.

Like the Englishman, you may be content to try a course of action once and if you don't find immediate gratification, never try it again. We must caution you, and encourage you, however, to continue to employ the recommendations and practice the exercises in this book. You will probably not meet success in your first few overtures, but you must keep working at refining your "people skills" so you can become more productive and bring greater harmony to your work environment.

Win-win outcomes are possible in every human encounter. But it is up to us to overcome the restraining forces, to reduce barriers so that we can achieve desirable outcomes. Displaying self-confidence among the unshakeably poised—and self-control among the acid-tongued—will enable us to work together in a spirit of cooperation and not competition.

Situation: At a brainstorming session, you offer an idea you believe has merit. The committee member responds, "That's the dumbest idea I've ever heard!" What would your reply be?

_____

_____

_____

_____

Situation: It is common knowledge around the office that you have won the state lottery. You are continuing to work by choice, but occasionally someone, prompted no doubt by jealousy, makes a remark such as, "Why should *you* care? You don't have to work for a living!" What would be a good response?

_____

_____

_____

_____

RECOMMENDATIONS

Not all of the following techniques will work all of the time. Nor will they work in every situation. However, we recommend trying as many as you can, as often as you can. In time, you will acquire confidence and competence in your ability to think well on your feet.

✔ Stand up for yourself. Remember that you have as much right as anyone else to be heard. Earn the respect of others by politely, but firmly, expressing your viewpoint. As Eleanor Roosevelt wisely observed, "No one can make you feel inferior without your consent."

Don't become too defensive (maybe there is some merit in what the "competitor" had to say). But don't over-apologize either. Say *something*, even if it is a neutralizing remark such as, "I can see you feel strongly about this. I respect that. But I'll ask you to respect the fact that other points of view are also possible."

✔ If the person is merely "expounding," listen carefully, without interrupting, to what he has to say. Often the competitor is merely seeking attention and once he has been given it, he will stop clamoring to be in the public eye. Of course, the longer he talks, the more time you have to prepare your defense and to reply in an intelligent, persuasive manner. To help you separate the "expounder" from the true "competitor," you should ask yourself these questions:

- Does the person have a legitimate complaint? Might I possibly react this way, given these circumstances?
- Is this typical behavior for this person?
- Is this truly an attack or merely a release of pent-up feelings?
- Am I over-reacting? Am I considering it hostile when it may be a simple disagreement or expression of a different point of view?
- Is the person attacking me or the information I am presenting?

Of course, if he continues non-stop, you may have to interrupt, but try to do so in a non-confrontational way. If he pays no attention to you, get his attention in any way you can. Stand up if you have to, or shout, or repeat one word over and over until he stops and yields the floor to you.

✔ If the competitor is attacking in a belligerent, belittling way, you will want to stop the attack and interrupt the flow of vitriol. You can tell him you will deal with him and with the problem at a later time. Explain that you sincerely wish to resolve the problem, but that you will only do so when the circumstances are conducive to the best possible discussion.

If you have command of the situation, you may wish to suggest a break at this point. Or end the meeting and ask him to remain after the others have left.

✔ Try humor if you can. It won't always work—nothing *always* works—but it often defuses a volatile situation as nothing else can.

✔ Acknowledge the merits of the competitor's claim, if, indeed, it does have merit. Sometimes people are so tired of being ignored that their anger escalates to the point of explosion. You may not, in fact, be the real target of the competitor's offensive behavior. He may not be consciously striving to make *you* feel or look bad. He may simply need to be heard.

You can pay the person a compliment, a sincere compliment, if it is deserved. Most people will feel too foolish to continue attacking after having received public recognition of the worth of their comments.

✔ If the person questions or casts doubt on information you have presented, ask him what evidence he has to support his charge. (You, of course, must have your own research or evidence to substantiate the claims you are making.) Ask for examples. Ask ''extensional'' questions that encourage the person to take the next step in the thinking process or that may help him to answer his own questions.

✔ Ask the person what you could do to satisfy her.

CUSTOMER SERVICE

Thinking well on your feet can help you convert a dissatisfied customer into a satisfied one. The rule to remember is an easy one: without your customer you would not have a job. Put yourself in the customer's shoes and try to imagine what the customer is thinking and what has led him or her to those thoughts.

Looking at every customer interaction from the customer's perspective will help you find the words to assure that customer you really are concerned about her needs, her expectations. You cannot help but evince sincerity if you think customer thoughts as you think on your feet. Keep your customer in the forefront of your brain. Treat her as *you* would wish to be treated. Serve the customer with pleasantness, offering suggestions and assurances that she deserves. She is, after all, why your company is in business.

We can respond professionally and caringly in our customer contacts if we have taken the time to learn what the customer truly expects. Armed with such knowledge, you will be better prepared to interact with the myriad of situations that your customers bring to you. You will be able to think on your feet and sound polished rather than dumbfounded, because you are guided always by the customer's interest.

Without knowing what your customers expect, it is hard for you to know if you have delivered satisfactorily. Record here what your customers' expectations are or what you believe them to be. (Note: The rapidity with which you answer these questions is a good indication of your ability to think on your feet. Mentally assess yourself on a 1–10 scale after you answer the question.)

_____

_____

_____

_____

_____

_____

_____

_____

_____

_____

1. What steps have you (or your company) taken to ensure that your assessment of customers' expectations is accurate?

_____

_____

_____

_____

_____

On a scale of 1–10, with 10 being highest, how satisfied are your customers with your company's products or services? _____

2. What evidence is there that the assessment is correct? (If there is no formal feedback system, what could be developed?)

_____

_____

_____

_____

_____

On a scale of 1–10, how developed is your feedback system? _____

3. Hundreds of thousands, perhaps millions of people go to work every day and do their jobs and do not give a single thought to the customer. In some companies, there is no formalized statement or philosophy regarding how customers are to be treated. Why do you think the customer is so often ignored?

_____

_____

_____

_____

(Now mentally assess your ability to think about these concerns.)

The Results of Poor Customer Treatment

You may have heard these customer-service slogans; they epitomize some companies' policies as far as customers are concerned.

"We try harder."
"Rule #1: The customer is always right. (Rule #2: If the customer is ever wrong, re-read Rule #1.)"
"Satisfaction guaranteed."
"The customer is king."

What is your company's policy regarding customer satisfaction (or, what do you think it should be)?

_____

_____

_____

_____

When customers are not satisfied, when they have not been dealt with correctly the first time, the seeds for losses are being sown. Here are the likely consequences of poor treatment of customers:

Unhappy customers. Technical Research Assistance Programs, Inc. (TARP) studies have found that angry customers who are not dealt with promptly end up costing the company more money in the long run. These customers tend to seethe over the situation and by the time they have called or written to the company president, they have made the original complaint seem much worse than it was. Thus, the longer it takes for the situation to be resolved, the more costly it becomes.

Wasted time. We wind up dealing with the customer issue twice instead of just once.

Lost opportunity for repeat business. TARP research has shown that disgruntled customers are twice as likely to report a bad experience to others as satisfied customers are to report a positive experience. So, not only has an opportunity for repeat business from a given customer been lost, we may also have lost untold customers who have been exposed to horror stories about our firm.

Wasted advertising dollars. Word-of-mouth, negative "advertising" stemming from customer dissatisfaction may be creating a poor reputation for our firm. The circulation of stories involving customer complaints may be offsetting the positive image that the company is trying to project.

A Customer Service Scenario
(Does it sound familiar?)

In the following scenario, you will have an opportunity to critique the way an employee of XYZ department store dealt with a customer's telephone complaint. While you may be tempted to think this dialogue a fabrication, it is based on an actual angry customer incident.

Employee: *XYZ.*

Customer: *My name is Sue Smith and I'm calling . . .*

Employee: *Hold, please.*

                [long pause]

Employee: *XYZ.*

Customer: *Yes. My name is Sue Smith and I'm calling to complain about a microwave I just bought in your store. After I paid for it, I was told . . .*

Employee: (interrupting) *What's the complaint?*

Customer: (starting to get angry) *I'm trying to tell you what the complaint is. After I purchased the item, I was told to go to "Customer Pick-up" and they would load it into my car.*

Employee: *So? That's our normal policy.*

Customer: *So when I got to "Customer Pick-up," I had to wait three minutes while the security officer talked on the phone about what she was serving for dinner that night. Then, when she finally turned to me, she grabbed the receipt out of my hand—didn't say a word, just grabbed the receipt and told another employee to put the microwave in my car.*

Employee: *Lady, I'm busy. What is your point?*

Customer: *My point is that I noticed the box was opened and when I told the security officer about it, she said it was company policy to open all boxes sent from the manufacturer to be sure nothing is missing.*

Employee: *So? That is our policy.*

Customer: *Well, when I got home and unpacked the box, I found that the instruction booklet and the warranty were missing.*

Does It Sound Familiar? (continued)

Employee: *Lady, what's the big deal? Just bring it back in the original box and we'll give you another one.*

Customer: *(angry now) Look. It took me 15 minutes to drive to the store in the first place and another 15 just to get the damn thing into my car. Now you're telling me I have to come back and start the whole process over again? What is your name?*

Employee: *(a little nervous at this point) Sorry. We are not allowed to give our names over the phone. Please hold.*

                    [The line goes dead.]

Customer: *(having redialed, finds herself speaking to the same operator) My name is Sue Smith. I just called to complain about the treatment I received and the fact that the microwave oven I purchased was missing the warranty. Let me speak to the service manager. I am very angry over this.*

Employee: *Sorry, the service manager is not in today.*

Customer: *Well, let me speak to whoever is in charge around there.*

Employee: *I guess that would be me.*

Customer: *Give me the name and address of the president of the company, dammit!*

Employee: *I don't have to listen to talk like that. (She cuts the connection.)*

How would you have handled this situation? The dialogue is reprinted below. Assume you were the XYZ employee and fill in the blanks with the appropriate comments.

Employee: _____

          _____

Customer: *My name is Sue Smith and I'm calling . . .*

Employee: _____

          _____

                    [long pause]

Employee: _____

          _____

Customer: *Yes. My name is Sue Smith and I'm calling to complain about a microwave I just bought in your store. After I paid for it, I was told . . .*

Employee: (interrupting) _____

_____

_____

Customer: (starting to get angry) *I'm trying to tell you what the complaint is. After I purchased the item, I was told to go to "Customer Pick-up" and they would load it into my car.*

Employee: _____

_____

_____

Customer: *So when I got to "Customer Pick-up," I had to wait three minutes while the security officer talked on the phone about what she was serving for dinner that night. Then, when she finally turned to me, she grabbed the receipt out of my hand—didn't say a word, just grabbed the receipt and told another employee to put it in my car.*

Employee: _____

_____

_____

_____

Customer: *My point is that I noticed the box was opened and when I told the security officer about it, she said it was company policy to open all boxes sent from the manufacturer to be sure nothing is missing.*

Employee: _____

_____

_____

_____

Does It Sound Familiar? (continued)

Customer: *Well, when I got home and unpacked the box, I found that the instruction booklet and the warranty were missing.*

Employee: _____

_____

_____

_____

Customer: (still angry) *Look. It took me 15 minutes to drive to the store in the first place and another 15 just to get the damn thing into my car. Now you're telling me I have to come back and start the whole process over again? What is your name?*

Employee: _____

_____

_____

_____

Customer: (having redialed, finds herself speaking to the same operator). *My name is Sue Smith. I just called to complain about the treatment I received and the fact that the microwave oven I purchased was missing the warranty. Let me speak to the service manager. I am very angry over this.*

Employee: _____

_____

Customer: *Well, let me speak to whoever is in charge around there.*

Employee: _____

_____

Customer: *Give me the name and address of the president of the company, dammit!*

Employee: _____

_____

RECOMMENDATIONS

✔ Sound sincerely interested in the other person's problems.

✔ As soon as you can, let the other person know you are taking notes on the conversation. At the very beginning, ask for the person's name, address, and phone number. For some reason, when people know they have been "identified," it diminishes the likelihood that they will be verbally abusive.

You should establish what you are doing with a sentence like this: "Excuse me for interrupting, Miss Smith, but before we go any further, I want to be sure I have your exact name and address so that I can share all the details with our Customer Service Manager. I'm going to take notes on what you tell me and will pass them along to him. Could I have your phone number, too? He will probably want to call you to assure you that we have taken steps to avoid this sort of problem in the future."

Note: There should be an established policy of what happens to complaints. If you are the first-line recipient, there is probably a second-line recipient as well. If that person does make phone calls to offer assurances, do say so. But don't assure the customer that a manager will be in touch if that is not policy or if there is little likelihood that the manager would actually make the call.

✔ If at all possible, don't put the person on hold. Listen patiently and let the customer explain what happened in her own words.

✔ Don't automatically denounce or condemn the person or department that seems to be at fault. Remember, you are only hearing one side of the story. Support the customer without criticizing the company. It's admittedly difficult, but you might say something such as, "I'm surprised and sorry to hear that. It is not the policy of XYZ to treat customers that way. I can assure you that we will investigate the situation further."

✔ Ask questions, if appropriate, so the customer will know you are sincerely interested in getting full details. Take good notes.

✔ Defend the company whenever you can. The customer may be upset about a policy without completely understanding why the policy was instituted. A rational explanation usually helps to mollify anger.

RECOMMENDATIONS (continued)

✔ Explain what you will do to rectify the situation. Do not make promises. Do not make extreme statements, for example, ''That security officer's behavior was inexcusable! He will be fired today!'' Do not say it will never happen again (because it might). Simply assure the customer that you will do everything possible to reduce the chances of such an occurrence happening again.

If you do not know what you are authorized to do via compensation, find out. Then, the next time you receive a similar complaint, you will be able to tell the customer exactly what the company will do to replace or repair the item. Some companies, in an effort to retain the customer, will send coupons or a small gift item as a means of extending their apologies for the incident.

✔ Do not be overly apologetic. In fact, if you do use the word ''sorry,'' try to express regret that the person feels as she does, rather than regret that your company was at fault. (This may not be the case.) Expressions such as ''I'm sorry you feel that way,'' or ''I can understand why you would be upset,'' or ''We would hate to lose a customer like you,'' can help build a rapport with the complainer without incriminating your company.

✔ If the customer is really irate, you do not need to subject yourself to any sort of abuse, especially if you were not the one who caused the problem in the first place. Don't simply hang up on the person. Instead, diplomatically suggest that the conversation take place later or ask if you can contact her at a later time.

✔ Stay calm. It will do no one any good if you become as irate as the customer. Remember, you are in business to serve customers, not to antagonize them.

✔ Try to end the conversation on a positive note. Do not repeat all the negatives the customer has cited. Rather, try to convey a sincere desire to help the customer solve her problem. Restate the essential facts of the situation. Explain that you will work to prevent the problem from occurring again. Thank the person for bringing the matter to your attention and express the hope that she will continue to do business with your firm.

Let's try a few situations that call for quick-wittedness on your part. As quickly as you can, record what you would say to these customers. (If you take the time to edit and revise your response, then you are not really "thinking on your feet.")

Situation: A customer calls to complain that he received the wrong order, for the third time this month! _____

_____

_____

_____

_____

_____

_____

Situation: A customer calls to complain that she was treated rudely by a receptionist. _____

_____

_____

_____

_____

_____

_____

Situation: A customer storms into your office, furious, because she has just spent an hour trapped in your elevator. _____

_____

_____

_____

_____

_____

EXERCISES

✍ 1

Over the next several weeks, use copies of this form to record all the "think-on-your-feet" situations in which you are involved. You may also use it to record your observations about others engaged in such situations. Watch for such situations wherever you are, whatever you are doing, even watching an expert being interviewed on the evening news, or the president answering reporters' questions. If you are *really* serious about developing your ability to think on your feet, you will keep such a log for the rest of your life.

1. Who were the people involved? (You need not give actual names, but rather, position titles such as "a secretary and her boss.")

_____

_____

_____

2. What were the circumstances?

_____

_____

_____

_____

3. What was the question or comment that forced one particular person to "think on his feet"?

_____

_____

_____

4. What was that person's response?

_____

_____

_____

_____

5. How would you assess that response?

_____

_____

_____

_____

6. What response would _you_ have given?

_____

_____

_____

_____

✍ 2

Make appointments with several individuals in fairly influential positions. They can be individuals in the upper echelon of your own company, or individuals with important roles in other organizations. (If you can't actually meet with the person, try to obtain the information in a telephone interview.)

Briefly explain that you are conducting a self-study research project on the topic of ''thinking on your feet.'' Ask people what advice they would give to someone trying to develop that skill. (Of course, if your question is answered right then and there, you will have an opportunity to see exactly how well the person _does_ think on her or his feet.)

✍ 3

First of all, make at least one copy of the following worksheet. (You will use it to compare your answers to the answers your friends or colleagues record on the same worksheet.) Next, have a stopwatch available. Then proceed to answer the question in the time allotted.

EXERCISES (continued)

1. Your boss, owner of a bathtub manufacturing facility, has just stopped by your desk. She has asked for your input on ways to improve bathtubs. She doesn't necessarily expect totally practical ideas, since this is just a brainstormed response she is seeking. How many bathtub-improvement ideas can you come up with in five minutes?

_____

_____

_____

_____

_____

_____

_____

_____

_____

_____

_____

_____

_____

_____

_____

_____

This exercise, by the way, is actually part of the interview process in at least one foreign company with plants in America.

2. Your boss, president of a cereal company, unexpectedly turns to you at the weekly staff meeting and asks for your reaction to an idea he has just had: putting fluoride in breakfast cereal in order to prevent tooth decay. What would you say?

_____

_____

_____

_____

_____

_____

3. Your secretary has just walked into your office, closed the door behind her, and confessed that (because she was pressured to get your activity report completed in time for your meeting) she was uncharacteristically rude to a caller who turned out to be the wife of a senior vice president. What will you say to your secretary? Write your answer immediately; assume she is standing there waiting for your response.

_____

_____

_____

_____

_____

_____

4. Your phone rings. You answer it. You gulp . . . it is the wife of the senior vice president, who _had_ been calling to invite you to a surprise birthday party for her husband. She is now calling to complain about your secretary's rudeness. Your reply?

_____

_____

_____

_____

_____

EXERCISES (continued)

4

At one point or another in our lives, most of us have had occasion to say, "If only I had thought of saying that at the time." We often come up with the perfect response—four days after we needed it. When we are under attack or being insulted, it is especially difficult to think clearly, for our brains seem to "freeze" when we are being scrutinized or pressured.

The first thing you must do is R–E–L–A–X. Self-talk and mentally assure yourself, "I can handle this. I've done it before." Then take a deep breath and say *something*. To stand there in shock allows the other person to know he has succeeded in leaving you dumbstruck. Even if you make a dignity-restoring comment like "I don't appreciate that remark," or "I don't think that was necessary," you will be further ahead than if you remain silent. Ideally, of course, you will be able to discharge a lucid volley of words that constitute an unforgettable retort.

Let's consider this example. Wellington Koo was a famous Chinese statesman and ambassador. He found, on more than one ambassadorial occasion, that Americans would note his ethnic features and make the assumption that he did not speak English very well. In 1921, he was in America, representing China at the Washington Conference.

At a state dinner during that time, he was seated beside a young woman who, having made her own assumption, turned to him and asked with a sweet and friendly smile, "Likee soupee?"

Koo just nodded, for he had no intention of carrying on a conversation on this level of articulation. After dinner, he was asked to address the audience, which he did for ten minutes—flawlessly. Upon his return to his seat, he turned to the young woman and spoke these words (Fill in the blank with a suitable comment.):

_____

Was your answer as good as Mr. Koo's? He turned to the young woman and asked, "Likee speechee?"

One of the secrets of a successful retort is to pick up a key word or pattern—a reference to an earlier remark—and weave it into the response whenever you can, as Mr. Koo did so successfully. Another example is the woman who had a good idea for an invention, and shared the idea with her husband. He—perhaps reacting with jealousy to her excitement—responded, ''You are acting as if you just put a man on the moon.''

Months later, after she sold the patent rights and received her first royalty check she made a copy of the check and left it on the kitchen table with this note, ''Will be gone for two weeks. I'm taking my first trip to the moon.''

Here are some real-world comments that were made to various people. Had you been in their shoes, what would your response have been?

1. ''Oh, what a pretty dress that is. I wish I could wear cheap clothes as well as you do.''

_____

_____

_____

_____

2. ''You have broken your fast for Lent!''

_____

_____

_____

_____

3. Someone who is very angry with your point of view declares, ''If I were married to you, I'd put poison in your coffee!''

_____

_____

_____

_____

EXERCISES (continued)

4. At a buffet luncheon, chicken is being served. You ask for the breastmeat and are told by the hostess that it is proper to ask for white meat or dark meat. To thank the hostess, you send her a splendid orchid the next day, with a thank-you note that reads:

_____

_____

_____

_____

5. At a dinner party with colleagues, you argue rather strenuously with one particular woman. She concludes the altercation by observing, with considerable scorn, that you are drunk. Your retort:

_____

_____

_____

_____

1. ''Oh, but you _do!_''
2. Erasmus replied to this reproach, ''I have a Catholic soul, but a Lutheran stomach.''
3. Winston Churchill replied, ''And if you were my wife, I'd drink it!''
4. Another Churchillian coup: his note read, ''I would be most obliged if you would pin this on your white meat.''
5. The final Churchill bon mot, ''And you, madam, are ugly. But _I_ shall be sober tomorrow.''

SECTION III

Speaking Before
An Audience

SPEAKING BEFORE AN AUDIENCE

The human brain starts working as soon as you are born and never stops until you stand up to speak in public. —Paul Cahill

---

The further your career progresses, the greater the chances are that you will be called upon to do some public speaking. Until you become comfortable with addressing a large group, you will never know the heady feeling that comes from having an audience respond to your ideas. Having them ''in the palm of your hand'' is an exhilaration like no other in the world.

Who is the best speaker you have ever heard? _____

What specific techniques or practices does this person use?

_____

_____

_____

_____

_____

_____

If the thought of standing before a group makes you apoplectic, try to analyze the reasons behind your fear. Record your thoughts here.

If, on the other hand, you actually *enjoy* giving a speech, try to recall what steps led you to this point of confidence.

_____

_____

_____

_____

_____

_____

SPEECHES

In one sense, prepared speeches are easier because you have had time to prepare. Unfortunately, you have also had time to get nervous about delivering them. By contrast, when you are unexpectedly called upon to "say a few words," or to deliver some "off-the-cuff" remarks, you don't have time to get nervous.

Here is a technique that will inject confidence into your veins and force the ice water out. We call it the **F–A–S–T** technique. Next time you are asked to speak extemporaneously, don't panic. Just think "FAST."

F = Focus
A = Amplify
S = Specify
T = Tie up

By *focus* we simply mean that you state the purpose or intent of your speech. You should tell your audience what the topic or main idea is and then go on to *amplify* that focus in one or two sentences. When you amplify you simply expand upon the focus.

You must then *specify* your main point with illustrations or examples, definitions or facts. Knowing that you have a logical plan to follow will help reassure you and will help calm those butterflies in your stomach.

Finally, you have to *tie up* your remarks with a summary that restates (in different words, if possible) the focus or thrust of your speech.

Now, let's practice using the FAST technique. Of the many topics you are knowledgeable about, pick one—it might be cooking or management or football or dogs or children.

Situation: Imagine that you are in the audience at the company's annual stockholder meeting. Your boss spots you and announces to the assembled group, "I see that we have an expert in our audience, a person who knows a great deal about _____ (the topic you selected on page 50)." She then beckons you to come up and address the group for four or five minutes. What would you say?

FOCUS: _____

_____

_____

_____

_____

AMPLIFY: _____

_____

_____

_____

_____

SPECIFY: _____

_____

_____

_____

_____

TIE UP: _____

_____

_____

_____

_____

MEETINGS

Meetings offer a terrific opportunity to gain visibility in your organization. And since power does not flow to invisible people, you need to contribute at meetings in such a way that you will indeed be noticed and remembered when promotions and performance appraisals and pay raises come around.

The whole secret to presenting yourself and your ideas well is to be prepared. If you truly wish to hone your ability to think on your feet, plan to present an idea at the next meeting you attend. In the beginning, present a suggestion or proposal that can be described in just a few minutes.

Over the next several weeks, answer the following questions and then rehearse your answers before you actually speak up at the meeting.

1. What is one suggestion I could make that would improve some work process?

_____

_____

_____

_____

_____

2. What would the benefit be to the company?

_____

_____

_____

_____

_____

3. What would the cost be to the company?

_____

_____

_____

_____

_____

4. Record here the names of the people who will probably be at the meeting. If there are over twelve, just record the names of the people who will probably react negatively to your suggestion.

a. _____

b. _____

c. _____

d. _____

e. _____

f. _____

g. _____

h. _____

i. _____

j. _____

k. _____

l. _____

5. Now go back to the names above and record what the likely reaction/objection of each person will be.

MEETINGS (continued)

6. For each reaction/objection you listed, record what you would say if you were called upon to respond on the spot.

a. _____

_____

_____

b. _____

_____

_____

c. _____

_____

_____

d. _____

_____

_____

e. _____

_____

_____

f. _____

_____

_____

g. _____

_____

_____

h. _____

_____

_____

i. _____

_____

_____

j. _____

_____

_____

k. _____

_____

_____

l. _____

_____

_____

Try to make at least one contribution to each meeting you attend. Use this form, or some variation of it, to help you prepare. You can't anticipate *every* question that will be thrown at you, but you will gain confidence through preparation and practice. And it is confidence that separates the best on-their-feet thinkers from their fall-flat-on-their-faces counterparts.

SOCIAL OCCASIONS

You will find many occasions in your life for celebration—both on and off the job—and where there is a celebration there is usually a toast offered. A toast that is memorable adds to the joy of the day. By comparison, a toast such as "Bottoms up!" (actually delivered by a best man at an elegant wedding) is probably best left unsaid.

The first time you are asked to make a toast, you may simply wish to deliver a memorized quotation instead of preparing your own eloquent remembrance of the occasion. There is nothing wrong with doing this; in fact, quotations such as these can lend a special significance to the event. You may even use the quote and then add an afterthought of your own.

"I drink to the general joy of the whole table."   —*William Shakespeare*

"A man hath no better thing under the sun, than to eat,
and to drink, and to be merry."   —*Ecclesiastes*

"A joy that's shared is a joy made double."   —*John Ray*

"[May] God, the best maker of all marriages,
Combine your hearts in one."   —*William Shakespeare*

"There is no more lovely, friendly and charming relationship,
communion or company than a good marriage."   —*Martin Luther*

"Grow old with me! The best is yet to be."   —*Robert Browning*

"Be not afraid of life. Believe that life is worth living,
and your belief will help create the fact."   —*William James*

There are many other quotations that can provide sparkle or splendor to toasts. If you enjoy wordsmithing, you might even take a famous quotation and add your own special twist to it. For example, Mark Twain observed that "Few things are harder to put up with than the annoyance of a good example." To which you might add, "Ladies and gentlemen, tonight we celebrate a man who—in Mark Twain terms—is the most annoying man in the whole company, precisely because he is the best example we could ever have of hard work, honesty, and integrity."

You may wish to keep a collection of toasts that you like and choose appropriate ones for those occasions when you are asked to say a few words about the person(s) or occasions being celebrated.

RECOMMENDATIONS

✔ No matter what the occasion, your remarks to an audience should be structured around a beginning, a middle and an end. Audiences need to envision a ''mental skeleton'' to which they can add the ''flesh'' of ideas as the talk progresses.

✔ Use quotations that are relevant to the occasion. Most quotable people can express their ideas much more elegantly than can the average person, so do not hesitate to quote them.

✔ Use familiar, everyday language to express your ideas.

✔ Rehearse at least ten times before you actually stand in front of a group. If you don't know specifically what you may be asked to address (a true on-your-feet situation), you should at least be armed with facts about the topic that will be discussed.

✔ Use transitions to connect your ideas.

✔ Weave an anecdote or story or real-life experience into your talk. Audiences respond better to concrete examples than to vague abstractions.

✔ Learn to pause occasionally to heighten the import of your words.

✔ Avoid the verbal crutches—the ''ums'' and ''ahs'' and ''you knows.'' For a full two weeks before your presentation, have a family member scream at you whenever you use one.

✔ Tape record yourself (at home) making the speech or answering a question at a meeting or delivering a toast. Listen to how you sound.

✔ If you think you will be overcome by nervousness, remind yourself that the people who will be sitting in that audience or sitting around the conference table are just human beings—they are no better or worse than you are.

If that doesn't work, imagine them sitting there in their underwear! That image will enforce the realization that they are just ordinary people.

If you are *still* nervous, tell yourself that there are a billion people in the world who couldn't care less about what you are going to say today!

EXERCISES

✍ **1**

Join the Toastmasters Club. Check the yellow pages phone directory. If there isn't one in your area, form one!

✍ **2**

Volunteer to speak to various organizations. The more you speak, the better you will become. The better you become, the more you will enjoy speaking before an audience. And the more you enjoy the process, the better you will be. It's a delicious cycle.

✍ **3**

Assume you are a nationally known figure in your field. You have been asked to deliver a commencement address at your alma mater. Write that speech.

✍ **4**

Now assume that on your way to the auditorium, a car goes out of control and nearly strikes you. You are shaken but safe. By the time you reach the podium, everyone in the audience has heard about your brush with death. You would like to make some reference to it before getting into your prepared remarks. How quickly can you revise the beginning of your speech to include some mention of the occurrence and then a segue to your topic?

_____

_____

_____

_____

A fictional politician, in a similar situation, revised his beginning to say, "As I was going to say, before I was so rudely interrupted. . . ." He then made mention of the fact that he had been born into a book-loving family, had spent all his adult days as a book-lover, reading and learning from books. He concluded by saying that he fully intended to die a book-lover—*but not today!*"

S E C T I O N

IV

Handling Difficult Questions

HANDLING DIFFICULT QUESTIONS

It is not every question that deserves an answer. —*Publilius Syrus*

Several years ago, the "Women in Film" organization held a symposium. The honored guest was an elderly, foreign film director whose mastery of the English language was halting at best. Nonetheless, the director delivered an impassioned and captivating speech and then opened the floor to questions.

An obviously intelligent, if somewhat prolix, young woman stood up and asked: "Can you tell me why the theme of bestiality inevitably appears in your films and whether or not you feel European audiences, as opposed to American, respond well to themes of that nature and if only the former, why don't you make films to which American audiences can respond with some degree of affinity and can embrace as we did with *cinema verite.* I'd also like to know how you would juxtapose the prototypical treatment of women depicted in European films with the American depiction of them." She spoke very rapidly—all of this directed at a person who was not able to follow the flow of ideas due to the language barrier.

In a masterful stroke, the director simply turned the question back to the young woman: "I would be happy to answer you. Now what was your first question again?"

The young woman, who had appeared so self-composed initially, suddenly lost control of that composure: she could not remember the first question she had asked! Red-facedly, she took her seat and other, simpler questions were then asked of the director by less garrulous people.

Some people simply *think* in complex, compound, convoluted sentences. They are not trying to impress others or to show off—they simply think in rather intricate syntactical patterns. Other people *are* trying to display their intelligence when they use 100-word-long sentences.

Whatever the reason, it is important to remember when you are faced with a situation like this that there is nothing wrong with asking to have the question repeated. Sometimes, even though you heard it the first time, it is wise to ask for a repeat because it will give you more time to formulate your own answer. If the question is a hostile one, however, it is not wise to have it repeated, for it only allows the heckler more power, more attention.

TYPES OF DIFFICULT QUESTIONS

Being able to categorize difficult questions somehow makes them less difficult. Certain questions have been put so often to so many people that they can actually be classified and labeled. Misery probably does love company and you can rest assured that you are not the only person who has ever been asked a tough question. If you recognize these questions, follow the recommendations, practice frequently and analyze both your successes and your failures, you should soon overcome your fear of the Question and Answer session. Some of the most frequently asked difficult questions follow.

1. THE "WHAT IF..." QUESTION

You may be pressured to answer a "What if..." question by someone who is persistent or who has perhaps heard a rumor and is urging you to confirm it. Such was the case with a bank chairman who was being asked if he would succeed a national political figure rumored to be resigning. "Would the Fed job interest you?" the reporter asked.

At first, the bank president was able to neatly sidestep the question by replying, "No one ever asked me."

The reporter persevered, "I'm asking."

The president would not be forced. He didn't wish to answer and was perfectly within his rights to decline a specific answer. What he did say was, "I once had a history professor who advised me never to answer questions in the subjunctive mood. It's probably a good idea."

Interviewers dislike such responses. Tomorrow, however, *they* will be off covering other stories. If you reveal privileged information when you are pushed, *you* may have to live with the negative ramifications of your answer for the rest of your life.

2. THE "TELL-US-WHAT-THE-BOSS-WILL-DO" QUESTION

Audience members or interviewers may feel that if you are behind the podium, serving as a spokesperson for the organization, then you must be privy to a great deal of behind-the-scenes information. Even if you are, you are usually not authorized to reveal it. A typical "Tell-us-what-the-boss/company-will-do" question sounds like this, "Is the chairman of the board really going to resign because of allegations of embezzlement?"

You can handle the situation very easily with a response such as "I cannot speak for the chairman," or "You will have to ask the chairman that question."

Some questioners are simply doing their job and are to be respected for asking tough questions and trying to discover the truth. Other questioners may just be curious or snoopy. No matter what the motive is, you will have to provide a response that protects both you and your organization.

3. THE "MACHINE-GUN" QUESTION

It may seem, in some circumstances, that the questioner is doing her best to mow you down with a rapid spray of questions, issuing vehemently from her machine-gun of a throat. Such questions are often belittling, often designed to hurt, often damaging, and often quite difficult to answer. A typical angry question would be "How could you permit this disgraceful situation to go on for six years?"

There are many possible ways to handle such a question. Not all of the approaches will work in all situations. But, as you acquire grace under pressure, you will also acquire an almost-intuitive sense of which approach works best with what sort of person.

- Try humor.

- Try admitting you made a mistake.

- Try going on the offensive. Ask the questioner, "What answer would satisfy you?" or "What would you like me to say?" or "What would you have done if you had been in this situation?"

- Try inviting the person to join you (and others, perhaps) on a committee to look further into the problem.

- Try defending yourself by explaining the cause or rationale behind the situation. However, a word of caution, this strategy often backfires and should only be used as a last resort. People who ask angry questions are usually in no mood to listen to logical explanations. Whatever you say will probably only provide them with more ammunition for further machine-gun verbal attacks.

RECOMMENDATIONS

✔ Establish a rapport with your audience as soon as you can—even before your speech begins. You can, for example, stand at the door and greet them as they come in. Introduce yourself and engage in small talk with a few people, if you like. Be considerate of their needs: make the room as comfortable as possible.

✔ If you spot a known troublemaker in the audience or if you sense someone is going to be difficult, do what you can to prevent the trouble before it starts. For example, experienced trainers can usually tell within the first half-hour if someone in the class is likely to be vocal or sarcastic or challenging. One way they cut off a potential challenger is to recognize a good idea the person has or perhaps allow the person a few minutes ''on stage'' to speak to the group.

✔ Try not to embarrass a heckler, even though he may be trying to embarrass you. Maintain your composure and your dignity, and you will stand a better chance of getting the audience on your side. Also, when a heckler is made to feel foolish, he is likely to become even more angry and his comments even more hostile.

✔ If you anticipate a really hostile audience, do not hold a Question and Answer period. Instead, pass out 3 × 5 cards before the meeting begins and collect them at the end of your presentation. Then you can rifle through them and answer only those questions you feel most comfortable with.

✔ Try to avoid saying, ''That's a good question.'' It implies that the other questions were not good.

✔ Cite statistics where appropriate in your answer. If you are thoroughly prepared, you should be able to refer to research studies and statistics quite easily. Such knowledge impresses an audience.

✔ Do not hesitate to use your own experience. It will help the audience relate to you and will make you seem more expert.

✔ Listen intently to the question. You may be able to handle it by not answering it, especially if it is not relevant. You might say, ''That's not germane to the issue here,'' or ''That would be like comparing apples and oranges.''

✔ Be thoroughly prepared for any question that might be asked of you. Learn more than you need to know. You will project a more professional tone if you are able to allude to additional data.

✔ If a hostile question appears to have generated considerable support from the audience and you think you might be outnumbered, try to postpone a full-fledged discussion until a later time. Otherwise, the opposition may get out of control.

✔ There *is* one thing you can do if you are truly nervous about your ability to handle difficult questions—have a "plant" in the audience. Ask a good friend to be there to help you out if necessary. Then, if an impossibly difficult question is foisted upon you, the "plant" in the audience can speak up to deflect attention from you. The plant might say, "I disagree with your point of view. You are attacking the speaker for something he has no control over." Or, "I'd like to respond to that if I could."

✔ Try to end the session after you have had a question to which you have been able to provide an intelligent, upbeat answer. You will then leave your audience with a favorable impression.

By contrast, if you say, "This will be the last question," and it is negative, the presentation will end on that discordant note.

EXERCISES

✍ **1**

Keep a log of difficult questions you hear being asked and exemplary answers you hear being given. If you find answers that are less than admirable, log in the answer *you* would have given.

✍ **2**

Have a friend prepare a list of ten really difficult, really disturbing questions. Do not look at the questions! Then, the next time you meet for coffee, have your friend ask you the questions. Think on your feet and answer the questions to the best of your ability, keeping the recommendations in mind. After you have answered all of the questions, ask another friend to do the same thing and start all over again.

Here are some questions to get you started. (Assume they were asked by someone you really like and whom you do not wish to offend.)

1. You haven't even been here three years! Why do you think you deserve this promotion over people who have been here five years and longer?

_____

_____

_____

_____

_____

2. Why did you invite the general manager to your house for Thanksgiving? Are you trying to win him over so he'll make your pay raise bigger than ours?

_____

_____

_____

_____

_____

3. You are telling us that we have to accept budget cuts and no raises this year. What sacrifices are *you* going to make? Are you going to give up your stock options this year, now that the company is in financial difficulty?

_____

_____

_____

_____

4. I heard you got this job because the manager is your brother-in-law. Is that true? (Assume, for the sake of this practice, that it is true.)

_____

_____

_____

_____

5. How much did you pay for your house?

_____

_____

_____

_____

6. I notice you wear an earring in your ear. Could I ask why?

_____

_____

_____

_____

7. How old are you?

_____

_____

_____

_____

EXERCISES (continued)

8. Is that necklace real gold?

_____

_____

_____

_____

9. This is really none of my business, but someone said you have been married three times. Is that true?

_____

_____

_____

_____

✍ **3**

Make interview appointments with people in your company who do a lot of public speaking. You may also wish to interview lecturers, politicians, minor celebrities—anyone who frequently stands before a group of people and permits them to probe his mind. Ask these questions:

- How do you handle difficult questions?
- What was the worst question/situation you ever faced?
- What kind of person is a typical heckler?
- Have you ever lost your temper when asked a difficult question?
- What advice can you give to someone who fears facing tough questions?

✍ **4**

At least once a week, as you are reading newspaper or magazine articles, write down (on separate 3 × 5 cards) one difficult question you would like to ask concerning the article. After you have collected at least 15 questions, invite two or three colleagues to have a lunchtime training session with you. Tell them the situation, ask the difficult questions and let each of them, in turn, answer them.

Afterwards, discuss who handled the questions most professionally and why you felt they did. They, in turn, can ask questions of you based on other articles as well. You might even invite an outside person to be the judge and decide who is the best extemporaneous speaker.

S E C T I O N

V

Developing Confidence

DEVELOPING CONFIDENCE

You gain strength, courage and confidence by every experience in which you really stop to look fear in the face. You are able to say to yourself, ''I lived through this horror. I can take the next thing that comes along. . . .'' You must do the thing you think you cannot do.   —Eleanor Roosevelt

There is a direct correlation between your confidence level and the competence others perceive you to have. There is also a direct correlation between your confidence level and your own perception of your own competence.

Of course, it is possible to be supremely self-confident and not know what you are doing. On the other hand, you can be extremely competent and still lack confidence. Ordinarily, though, the more confidence you have in your abilities, the more those abilities can be and are being and have been developed. And the more they are developed, the more self-confident you become. When you have utter faith in yourself and the direction in which you are moving, you can then lead others to the accomplishment of great things. And the more empowered you and they are, the more confidence you acquire.

Graphically, the Confidence Cycle looks like this:

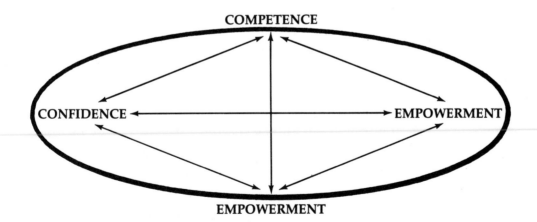

SELF-EMPOWERMENT ANALYSIS

On a scale of 1–5, with 5 being highest, rate your degree of comfort in performing each of these actions, most of which will require on-the-spot thinking. Without deliberating very much, record what you would say in these situations.

1. Everyone at the meeting, including your boss and your boss's boss, has expressed approval for a plan of action. You are the last person to give an opinion and your opinion is that the plan will not work. How comfortable would you be in expressing the only dissenting vote? (Circle the number that best reflects your degree of comfort.)   1 – 2 – 3 – 4 – 5
What would you say?

_____

_____

_____

_____

_____

2. How comfortable are you about asking to see your boss without apologizing for taking up her time?   1 – 2 – 3 – 4 – 5   What would you say?

_____

_____

_____

_____

_____

3. You have just seen the person you most admire in the entire world being seated near you in a restaurant. How comfortable would you be in asking for her autograph?   1 – 2 – 3 – 4 – 5   What would you say?

_____

_____

_____

_____

_____

4. At a social gathering, someone has just told a joke you find offensive. How comfortable would you be in telling the person you did not appreciate his humor?   **1 – 2 – 3 – 4 – 5**   What would you say?

_____

_____

_____

_____

_____

5. How comfortable would you be in complaining to a doctor or lawyer about the high price she had charged?   **1 – 2 – 3 – 4 – 5**   What would you say?

_____

_____

_____

_____

_____

B. C. Forbes has observed that "Business places no premiums on shrinking violets. Employers prefer [wo]men who have self-assurance, forcefulness, go-aheadness—[wo]men who know their job and know that they know it." The five questions above (and additional ones in the Exercises section) are meant to prompt you to think about your "shrinking violet" or "blooming violet" behaviors. If you scored lower than 20 on the analysis, you will want to pay particular attention to the following recommendations for increasing your sense of self-worth.

RECOMMENDATIONS

✔ Find someone in your organization whom you consider a true leader. Compare his communicating style to your own. When you note specific ways in which he is a better communicator than you, study what he says and attempt to imitate some of the most powerful aspects of his style. If possible, develop a mentor relationship with him.

✔ Don't agonize over your communication failures. Don't give yourself daily verbal beatings for mistakes that you have made. Learn from your errors but don't hold yourself hostage to memories of embarrassing or awkward times when you had to think on your feet. Move forward without guilt or blame or shame.

✔ Self-talk. Whenever you *do* think on your feet especially well, compliment yourself. Make note of what you said, of how your audience responded, of what you might have done to make your performance even better.

✔ Ask for feedback. Have several friends/colleagues who are concerned about your well-being, evaluate each of your attempts to think on your feet.

✔ Seek out every possible opportunity to think on your feet. Begin in small ways, with strangers. Volunteer to teach a Sunday school class or a Girl or Boy Scout troop. Talk to civic groups seeking new speakers. Develop your skills of response and repartee. Whenever possible, have one of your evaluating friends/colleagues with you. Discuss your "performance" afterwards. In time, you will be eager to try more challenging situations. Think about doing some training at work; volunteer to make a presentation at the next staff meeting. Always distribute evaluation forms at the end of your sessions. The comments from those who made you think on your feet (or who watched you think on your feet) will enable you to maximize your skills.

✔ Keep paper and pencil with you as you watch television, especially interviews with recognized national and international figures. Become sensitized to the specific techniques they employ to give quick but meaningful replies to unanticipated questions/circumstances.

EXERCISES

✍ **1**

Here are additional questions to help you analyze the extent of your willingness to interact with individuals who require you to think on your feet. MAKE THREE COPIES OF THE QUIZ. Again, you will rate yourself on a scale of 1–5 in terms of your comfort in dealing with these people or situations. Tally your score. Three, six, and nine months from now take the quiz again. Compare your scores to today's score. If you do not see much progress, it will be up to you to get more practice. The saying about practice leading to perfection may be trite, but it really is true!

1. How comfortable would you be in confronting someone you suspect of petty theft?   1 – 2 – 3 – 4 – 5

2. How comfortable would you be in explaining to a subordinate why she was passed over for promotion?   1 – 2 – 3 – 4 – 5

3. How comfortable would you be in dealing with malicious rumors being spread about you?   1 – 2 – 3 – 4 – 5

4. How comfortable would you be in having your authority challenged by a subordinate?   1 – 2 – 3 – 4 – 5

5. How comfortable would you be in asking for a refund on a defective product?   1 – 2 – 3 – 4 – 5

6. How comfortable would you be in reprimanding children visiting you with their parents?   1 – 2 – 3 – 4 – 5

7. How comfortable would you be in reminding an acquaintance she owes you money?   1 – 2 – 3 – 4 – 5

8. How comfortable would you be in refusing to do a favor for a friend?   1 – 2 – 3 – 4 – 5

EXERCISES (continued)

9. How comfortable would you be in admitting you made a mistake after you had insisted you were correct?   1 – 2 – 3 – 4 – 5

10. How comfortable would you be in refusing to do something your boss has asked of you, because you find it unethical?   1 – 2 – 3 – 4 – 5

✍ 2

Select at least five of the above scenarios and "write" on your feet—that is, as quickly as you can, write down what you would say if you were in the situations described above.

✍ 3

Read at least one book on leadership, public speaking or verbal self-defense.

✍ 4

Develop an action plan or a five-year-goal program. Specifically, you must record what your intended goal or aim or purpose is. You must also tell the steps leading to that goal and the dates by which you intend to reach each milestone on your journey.

SECTION

VI

Summary

SUMMARY

The essense of humanness is our language capability. A leader has only his or her language (the language of words and consistent, supporting deeds) as a "tool." To say that language is everything for the leader is not overstatement. It is fact.   —Tom Peters

---

Thinking well on your feet is an amalgamated ability. It is the result of many factors: your education, your upbringing, your vocabulary, your experience, your observations, etc. No one was born with this ability. The people you admire for their quick-wittedness have worked hard to develop that ability. If it is important to you to possess that skill, you must work until you do.

The examples, situations, recommendations and exercises in this book will help you attain your goal of thinking on your feet without putting them in your mouth. But they can only help if you are actually working with them. Engage others to help you. Compare your answers with theirs. Ask them for feedback.

Keep your eyes and ears open and sensitize yourself to both the content and context of answers given to questions that require people to think on their feet. The same questions will elicit different responses from different people. Whether *your* response falls into the brainless or braininess category will depend not on the thought you are trying to express, but rather, on the words you use to express that thought.

INTERVIEWS

Employment interviews are costly; therefore, you must be prepared for probing questions. Interviewers are not necessarily trying to make you feel pressured. More likely, they are trying to value the cost of the interview process by going beneath the surface to learn more about how well you think, how well you handle unanticipated situations, how well you maintain your composure.

INTERVIEWS (continued)

The best way to succeed in these interviews is to be prepared:

- Read a book on the interview process.

- Learn all you can about the company and the job.

- Go through several practice sessions with a friend.

- Video or audio tape yourself in a practice session.

- Go on as many job interviews as you can, even for jobs you may think are beyond your reach. With every one, you will be gaining valuable experience that you can use for present *and* future job-hunting situations. You will also be gaining self-confidence.

- When you go to the interview, have with you all the documents and information you may be asked for.

- Expect the unexpected. You may not have to deal with it, but if you expect to be asked difficult, penetrating questions, you will be able to handle them more easily than if you are caught off guard.

Preparation is the operative word in media interviews as well. Prior to the actual interview, arrange as many ''small'' interviews as you can. These might be interviews with a high school, college or local newspaper reporter. You can contact local talk show hosts or community service cable programs or college radio stations. Be resourceful. Give as many interviews as you can with as many media as you can before the all-important interview.

Recognize and congratulate yourself for these efforts. Remind yourself that you are gaining both competence and confidence in each of these preparatory steps. When you give an especially clear or memorable reply, make note of it. Commend yourself on your increasing verbal power. Remember Confucius's words: ''Without knowing the force of words, it is impossible to know men.'' In a similar vein, it is written in Job 6:25, ''How forcible are right words.''

COMMUNICATING WITH COLLEAGUES AND CUSTOMERS

So many difficulties encountered in our personal and professional lives can be traced to misunderstandings. There are aspects of the communication process to bear in mind in order to prevent future miscommunications:

1. Communication is irreversible.
2. Communication is constant.
3. Communication connects (or dis-connects) us.
4. Communication can always be improved.

There is a plethora of ways for dealing with the communication problems that may arise between you and a colleague. Essentially, you can operate from one of three foundations: niceness, nastiness or neutrality. Only you will be able to determine which style will work best with which individual under which circumstances.

But, no matter which style you select, you and your colleague must both remember why you have come into each other's lives: Keep in mind that you were each hired for your ability to make a contribution to the organization. That purpose must be uppermost in both your minds. If your communication conflict is preventing you from doing your job efficiently, then you must find a way to resolve the differences. Remember that your interaction is a small part of the larger picture of organizational success.

The very same reminder should influence your interactions with customers. Dissatisfied customers can cost your company a great deal of money:

- They will tell others about their dissatisfaction, creating a loss of public image as well as the loss of potential future customers.

- The unhappy customers themselves may stop doing business with your firm. If this happens, you have lost an opportunity for repeat business.

- Dealing with the customer means neglecting other work because you have to take time to deal with a person who should have received satisfaction the first time around.

COMMUNICATING WITH CUSTOMERS (continued)

Listen attentively when customers call to complain. Take notes on what they are saying and ask questions to assure them that you are truly interested in what they are saying. Try not to put them on hold or to interrupt. Do not go overboard in condemning your company. (One customer service representative actually told a customer, ''Oh, we get calls like this all the time. You are the sixth person today who has called to complain about this.'') Remain poised and professional throughout the interaction. Explain what will be done next and thank the customer for her time. Always try to end the conversation on an upbeat note.

SPEAKING BEFORE AN AUDIENCE

Think about the fact that every time you open your mouth to speak, you are letting others see into your brain. If the words you speak are well-organized, others will assume you have a fully functioning brain. If, on the other hand, you mumble and stumble, your audience will begin to think other thoughts rather than attend to what you are saying.

One indirect way to develop your speaking skills is to watch and listen to what the best do and then employ some of the same strategies they use. Practice incorporating the best from the best into your own speaking style.

A more direct way is the ''F–A–S–T'' technique. Use it when you are unexpectedly called upon. State the Focus of your brief speech—its purpose or the topic. Then Amplify on that focus in a sentence or two. Next, Specify. Give specific examples or details about the main idea or focus of your talk. Finally, Tie up. Conclude your remarks by restating your main point(s).

Practice speaking up at meetings. Perhaps you could even make it a goal to offer one suggestion or opinion at every meeting you attend for the next three months. By the end of that period, you should be ready to set another goal: make a proposal about some improvement to the processes involved in your work at least once every three months. These proposals, of course,will require more forethought, more research and more explanation than merely making a suggestion. But if your ideas are basically sound and if you can defend them well, you will be enhancing the professional image you convey.

Memorize a few quotations that will fit any social occasion at which you may be asked to give a toast in honor of the celebrants or the event. When you become more skilled, you can add a personal touch in your own words.

No matter what the occasion, though, use appropriate language, anecdotes, examples and pauses.

HANDLING DIFFICULT QUESTIONS

There are many categories of difficult questions, but three that are quite popular are the "What If . . . ," the "Tell-Us-What-the-Boss-Will-Do," and the "Machine-Gun" questions. Handling yourself with aplomb and the questions with ease depends on your ability to think before you speak. Be careful about the impact your words will have on the audience and choose another answer if you see the red flag flying above your first thought. Better to pause for a few seconds than to live forever with damaging remarks.

Hecklers in an audience are part of every speaker's nightmare. Actually, you should be grateful for them as they will strengthen your ability to think quickly on your feet. You will probably not do well in coping with hecklers the first few times, but each time you will get better. There will always be more speeches for you to give—many of them much more critical to your success than the first few heckler-hexed speeches.

As your confidence builds, so will your skills in deflecting the sting of the heckler's barbs. Some general suggestions include trying to disarm the complainer by acknowledging her or giving her a chance to be heard or complimenting her on an idea or presentation of facts. Try your very hardest not to antagonize the heckler, for such a response will usually only incite her further.

If you truly fear there will be questions that will knock you off your feet, and thus render you unable to think, have the audience write their questions on 3 × 5 cards and then answer only those with which you feel comfortable. Keep your answers brief and try to end on a positive note.

DEVELOPING CONFIDENCE

As you have progressed through this book, you have been developing confidence. Each time you tried one of the practices, your experience and expertise grew a little bit. As they grew, so did your competence. Possessing both confidence and competence empowers you to accomplish new deeds. And, with each accomplishment, your confidence grows and the cycle continues.

You can boost your confidence further by identifying someone within the organization who thinks exceptionally well on his feet. Learn from that person and seek to have him or her become your mentor, if possible. Obtain feedback from others who are sincerely interested in your well-being.

Realize that not all of your attempts will be successful. However, you can profit from those that are not and then move on to the next challenge without flagellating yourself with the whips of guilt or blame or self-accusation. If anything, you should be engaging in self-talk, complimenting yourself on the things you did well and assuring yourself that the things you did not do well will be improved upon the next time. And there will always be a next time— an opportunity to show the world that you can indeed think on your feet!

We hope you enjoyed this book. If so, we have good news for you. This title is part of the best-selling *FIFTY-MINUTE*™ *Series* of books. All *Series* books are similar in size and identical in price. Several are supported with training videos (identified by the symbol **Ⓥ** next to the title).

FIFTY-MINUTE Books and Videos are available from your distributor. A free catalog is available upon request from Crisp Publications, Inc., 1200 Hamilton Court, Menlo Park, California 94025.

FIFTY-MINUTE Series Books & Videos organized by general subject area.

Management Training:

Human Resources & Wellness (continued):

Communications & Creativity:

Customer Service/Sales Training:

Small Business & Financial Planning:

Adult Literacy & Learning:

Career/Retirement & Life Planning: